How to Create Math Experts With
Base Ten Blocks

Lyle Lee Jenkins

I0541831

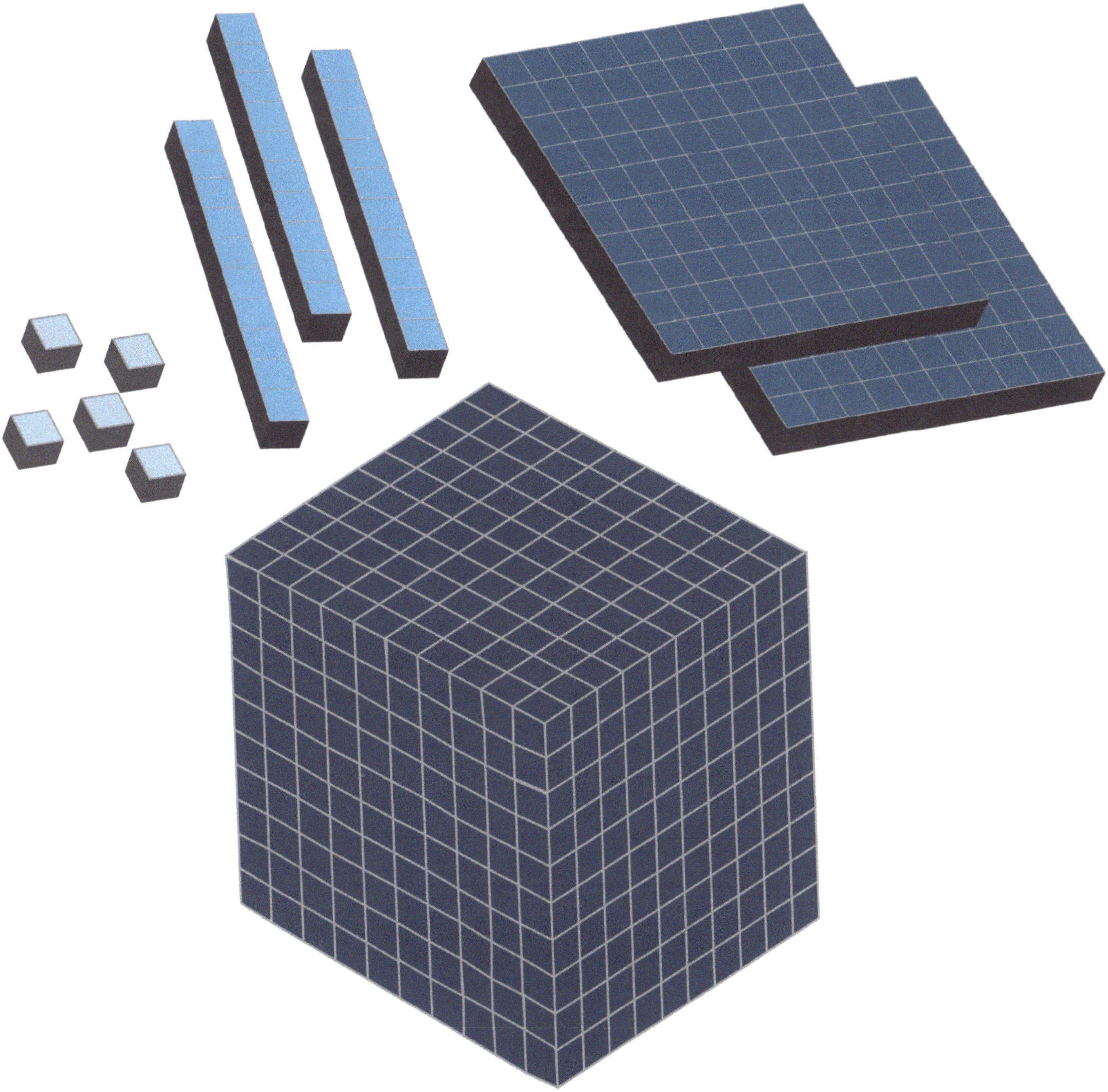

Perfect School Collection™

To contact author about booking keynotes, workshops or bulk material orders visit LtoJ.net/Contact

ISBN: 978-1-956457-51-3

Book Design & Graphics: Christy Courtright, Christy's Customs LLC
Quality Assurance Manager: Kelly Lippert
Publishing Consultant: Martha Bullen, Bullen Publishing Services
Distribution Coordinator: Maggie McLaughlin
Printed in the United States of America

The Perfect School Collection™

How to Create a Perfect School by Lyle Lee Jenkins

How to Create a Perfect Home School by Lyle Lee Jenkins and Kelly Hawkinson Lippert

Perfect School Collection™ Resources

How to Create Math Experts series by Peggy McLean and Lyle Lee Jenkins

How to Create Math Experts with Fluency Quizzes by Peggy McLean and Lyle Lee Jenkins

How to Create Math Experts with Math Standards Quizzes by Peggy McLean, Laura Hayes and Lyle Lee Jenkins

How to Create a Math Foundation for Future Math Experts by Lyle Lee Jenkins

How to Create Language Experts with Literary Terms series by Codi Hrouda and Emma McInerney with Lyle Lee Jenkins

How to Create Bible Experts: Genesis to Revelation by Richard Douglas Junior Jenkins with Lyle Lee Jenkins

Young Readers

Bible Patterns for Young Readers series by Lyle Lee Jenkins

Aesop Patterns for Young Readers series by Lyle Lee Jenkins

Young Authors

Wordless Books for Young Authors series by Jim Chansler and Lyle Lee Jenkins

Special Projects

All About Henry: Rich Widower of Savannah Valley by Lyle Lee Jenkins

Contents

Introduction

PEGGY MCLEAN AND LYLE LEE JENKINS created a series of elementary math books to offer teachers proven resources for helping children master essential math concepts. Each book guides children to gain powerful lifelong math insights. Confidence builds more and more as children increase their math skills and knowledge from a young age. *How to Create Math Experts with Base Ten Blocks* is true to its title. Adults and children are amazed at what they learn from this powerful collection of four different blocks.

The book's subtitle, Constant Thrill from Success, does not mean immediate thrill or immediate success. When people are intrinsically motivated, they work hard, and the thrill comes from the learning. The aim is for students to be 100% engaged and love learning. The biggest thrill usually comes from a struggle over several days to finally solve a problem.

How to Create Math Experts with Base Ten Blocks is included within *The Perfect School Collection™* because it is an immense help in preserving intrinsic motivation. Lyle Lee Jenkins defines a perfect school as one in which the intrinsic motivation children bring with them to kindergarten is maintained for the next 12 years.

The metaphor of a tree with roots illustrates the process of children developing new skills. Images of trees rarely include the roots because they are hidden from view. However, we all know that if the roots die, it won't be long until the visible tree dies. John Hattie's "skill, will and thrill" learning model captures the thoughts behind the tree with roots. The visible tree is the math skill to be learned with Base Ten Blocks. The invisible roots represent the will and the thrill maintaining students' natural love of learning. When students' natural love of learning (intrinsic motivation) is destroyed, it is not very long before the visible tree (skills) falters and dies. That is why math skills must be learned in such an exciting way that children's intrinsic motivation is maintained at a very high level!

Ask adults and high school students to estimate how many high school students are as excited about school learning as they once were as kindergartners. The research shows that 5 to 8% of students keep this love of learning for 13 years of K-12 education. We can do better. *The Perfect School Collection™* books will greatly increase this percentage.

Children can play with hammers, screw drivers, and levels, but adults do not call these objects toys. Children can also play with Base Ten Blocks, but it would be a mistake to call them toys; they are tools just like rulers, compasses and protractors. In fact, Base Ten Blocks are one of the most powerful tools ever invented to give children a solid understanding of all operations with whole numbers.

The thrill of learning does not come from remembering rules and formulas often taught in math and phonics. It comes from children figuring out solutions on their own.

As mentioned earlier, the problems in *How to Create Math Experts with Base Ten Blocks* might not be solved instantly. When children are stumped and have no more energy for the task at hand, we suggest they move on to something else. We all know that solutions to adult problems often occur when not thinking directly about the problem. The solution can "pop into our heads" while in the shower, driving the car, or while we are on a walk or run. The same is true for children. While riding a bike, lying in bed or sitting in the back seat of the car, children can have an "aha moment" and can hardly wait to get a hold of the Base Ten Blocks and see if their "aha" is correct. When it is, we call this thrilling success.

Thrill does not come from an adult placing a check mark by a problem that is incorrect. When an adult is looking over a student's work, the adult should place a "c" by correct answers and a simple dot by incorrect ones. The dot means temporarily wrong. When the children correct the mistake, the "c" covers up the dot, and all problems on the page have the "c." A paper with all "c's" can be proudly shared with parents and other important people in a child's life. Constant thrill from success will become your and your students' reality with *How to Create Math Experts with Base Ten Blocks*.

Getting Started

How to Create Math Experts with Base Ten Blocks starts with place value as the foundation and proceeds onto square and cube roots. Every explanation requires the use of the Base Ten Blocks. Adults are amazed at how much math elementary age children can truly understand once they experience the use of the blocks with each new application. In fact, adults continually state, "Now I understand what my childhood teachers were trying to get me to learn."

PLEASE do not rush the movement from using the blocks to only pencil and paper math. Children know that adults do not carry blocks around in their purses and pockets and naturally strive to solve problems without blocks. The difference with a block foundation is the children are not trying to remember rules, but they have the pictures of their blocks in their heads as they attempt to solve problems without any blocks.

There is no order for the problems and explanations in *How To Create Math Experts with Base Ten Blocks*. Start with division if you desire. Because books have page numbers it is assumed that students must complete every page before moving onto the next page in the book. Skip around to learn what looks interesting. Children will remember more if they cycle back to complete the pages they started earlier.

We have all been taught that a problem with thousands and hundreds is more difficult than a problem with only ones and tens. That is a false idea when using blocks. What makes a problem more difficult is regrouping, not place value.

Easy problem:

Harder Problem:

$$
\begin{array}{r}
1346 \\
+\ 2312 \\
\hline
\end{array}
$$

$$
\begin{array}{r}
85 \\
+\ 26 \\
\hline
\end{array}
$$

The easy problem has no regrouping, and the harder problem requires trading ones for one 10-block and then trading ten 10-blocks for one 100-block. The structure of the sample problems minimizes the number of 1-blocks and gradually introduces more regrouping. All the problems in the books are chosen for their ease with blocks. For example, 7 x 8 is difficult with blocks as 56 blocks are needed. An easy problem with blocks is 11 x 11 as it only takes 4 blocks – one 100-block, two 10-blocks and one 1-block. Also, the problems often have patterns for children to notice. The best synonym for math is patterns and children quickly learn this.

Not only do children need to know how to add, subtract, multiply and divide, they need to know what questions these four operations can answer. It turns out there are eight basic questions they answer and *How to Create Math Experts with Base Ten Blocks* is organized around these eight questions. The Base 10 Blocks will be used to teach children about all eight questions and create an avenue to compute without the blocks. The transition from blocks to pencil and paper computation is gradual and at different paces for each child.

The steps are:

1. Learn how to complete the computation with the blocks

2. Complete some problems with blocks and some without blocks

3. Complete most problems without blocks but get stuck sometimes. When this happens say to the child, "Ask the blocks what you are missing and explain what you learned." I know this sounds crazy, but the students then return to the blocks and can explain to the adult what step they missed.

4. Students are competent with pencil and paper computation but will visualize the blocks as they complete their work.

The eight questions for arithmetic are:

1. Addition: How much are these items all together?

2. Subtraction: How much is left after we take away this much?

3. Subtraction: How much larger (heavier, smaller, stronger, etc.) is this than that?

4. Multiplication: If we do something more times, how much is this all together?

5. Multiplication: If I know the length and the width, how much is the area?

6. Division: If I divvy up what I have into equal groups, how much in each group?

7. Division: If I subtract over and over how many times before completely gone?

8. Division: If I know the area and the width or length, what is missing measurement?

We are accustomed to thinking that arithmetic must be learned in the order of +, -, x, ÷ but this is not necessary. Once place value is understood by the students, they are ready to explore all four operations with all eight of the questions. Because books have page numbers and the questions have numerals from 1 to 8, it can be assumed that students will learn them in the printed order. Please do not. There is no order to learn these problems. The student can select a problem from any page, or an adult can say, we haven't done any from this page yet. Let's dive in now. I do not suggest that the students complete all the problems on any one page in one setting. The concepts will become more fixed in the students' mind if they skip around from concept to concept gradually completing all the problems.

ADDITION

Addition is the simplest of the questions math can solve. How much is it all together? The page starts off with problems that do not require the students to exchange ten 1-blocks for one 10-block, ten 10-blocks for one 100-block or ten 100-blocks for one thousand block. The term most often used for this trading is regrouping: a bunch of blocks are regrouped into a larger block.

Write questions answered by adding together 2 or more things. 123 + 125 = 248

Build both numerals with the Base Ten Blocks. Next put all blocks into one pile. Record the number of 1-blocks, then number of 10-blocks, number of 100-blocks and finally the number of 1000-blocks.

ADDITION WORKSHEET
YOUR TURN!

```
   4 5          8 3
 + 5 4        + 1 6
```

```
   2 7          1 2 5
 + 7 2        + 1 2 3
```

```
   3 1 5        1 2 0 7
 + 6 8 4      +   3 1 2
```

```
   1 7            2 3
 + 2 3          + 1 7
 _____         _____


   2 4            2 5
 + 1 7          + 1 7
 _____         _____


   2 5            2 5
 + 2 5          + 7 5
 _____         _____
```

```
    2 1 5 8          1 1 1 5
  + 1 4 4 1        + 1 5 5 5
  ---------        ---------


    1 2 4 7          1 0 4 7
  + 1 3 4 2        + 1 9 2 4
  ---------        ---------


    1 1 2 3            3 4 9
  +   3 1 7        +   6 5 2
  ---------        ---------
```

ADDITION WORKSHEET
LET'S TRY EVEN MORE EVEN MORE YET!

```
  6 5 3          4 0 7
+ 3 4 9        + 5 9 3
```

```
  5 5 5          6 6 6
+ 5 5 5        + 6 6 6
```

```
  7 7 7          4 4 4
+ 7 7 7        + 4 4 4
```

SUBTRACTION BY TAKING AWAY

The first concept for subtraction is taking away something smaller from something larger. The first problems on the next page are simply taking away the blocks and writing the answer. Next, the problems require one of the 10-blocks to be traded for ten 1-blocks in order to have enough to take away. This trading is often called regrouping. As the problems become harder there are several regroupings necessary.

Write questions answered by taking something smaller from something larger.

 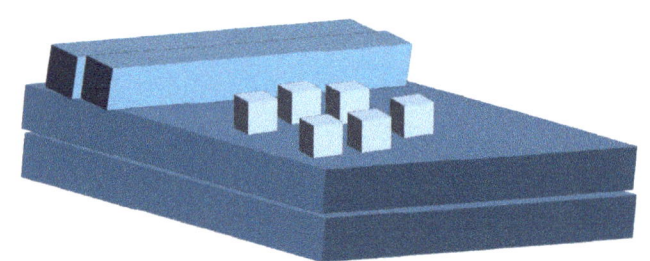

For the problem of 378 - 152, first we build the top number of 378 and then take away two 1-blocks, five 10-blocks, and one 100-block. Left over is shown in the picture at the right: six 1-blocks, two 10-blocks and two 100-blocks for an answer of 226.

```
  3 7 8              4 1 8
- 1 5 2            - 2 1 6
```

```
  5 9 8            1 2 5 8
- 3 3 3            -   2 5 8
```

```
  5 9 8              5 9 8
- 1 1 1            - 2 2 2
```

SUBTRACTION BY TAKING AWAY WORKSHEET
LET'S TRY SOME MORE!

```
   2 0          2 1
 - 1 5        - 1 5
 _____       _____



   2 2          2 3
 - 1 5        - 1 5
 _____       _____



   2 4          5 4
 - 1 4        - 1 4
 _____       _____
```

SUBTRACTION BY TAKING AWAY WORKSHEET
LET'S TRY EVEN MORE!

```
  1 2 4 7          2 1 5 8
- 1 1 3 5        - 2 1 3 7
_____        _____
```

```
  1 2 4 2          2 1 5 5
- 1 1 3 5        - 1 1 1 7
_____        _____
```

```
  1 1 6 5          1 4 2 7
- 1 1 3 9        -   3 2 5
_____        _____
```

SUBTRACTION BY TAKING AWAY WORKSHEET
LET'S TRY EVEN MORE YET!

```
  1 2 6 5          1 4 2 1
- 1 1 5 9        -   3 2 2
```

```
    1 0 0          1 0 0 0
-     1 5        -   3 1 5
```

```
  2 0 0 0          3 0 0 0
-   3 1 5        -   3 1 5
```

SUBTRACTION BY COMPARING

The second concept for subtraction is comparing something larger to something smaller. An example is, "How much taller is this chair than that chair?" For comparison subtraction students build both numerals – the larger one and the smaller one. Both numerals are built side by side. Add blocks onto the smaller one until both stacks are the same size. The answer is how much was added to make the blocks the same size.

For the problem 1000 - 800, the question is how much bigger is 1000 than 800. Place 800 next to the 1000 block and count how many blocks it takes for the two piles to be even.

The answer is 200 because two one-hundred blocks must be added to make two piles the same.

SUBTRACTION BY COMPARING WORKSHEET
YOUR TURN!

```
  1 0 0          1 0 0
-   2 0        -   8 0
_____    _____


  1 0 0 0        1 0 0 0
-   8 0 0      -   5 0 0
_____    _____


  1 0 0          3 0 0
-   9 0        - 1 0 0
_____    _____
```

SUBTRACTION BY COMPARING WORKSHEET
LET'S TRY SOME MORE!

```
  1 0 0 0          1 0 0 0
-     5 0        -   9 9 5
```

```
  1 0 0 0            5 0 0
-   8 5 0        -   4 7 5
```

```
    2 0 0            1 5 0
-   1 6 0        -   1 2 5
```

```
    800              700
  - 200            - 200
  ─────            ─────


    600              500
  - 200            - 200
  ─────            ─────


   2000             2000
  -  600           -  800
  ──────           ──────
```

MULTIPLICATION BY REPEATED ADDITION

The first concept for multiplication is repeated addition. An example multiplication problem with repeated addition is, "If there are 12 doors in the house and each door has 3 hinges, how many hinges all together?" We multiply 12 times 3 to obtain the answer of 36. In the problems that follow, students are to build the top number with the blocks and build the same number over and over based upon the number below. For example, if the problem is 235 x 3 = the student builds 235 three times and then puts all the blocks into one pile. When the student recognizes there are too many 1-blocks, then ten of them are traded for a 10-block. Now the students see there are too many 10-blocks and so they must be traded for a 100-block, giving a final answer of 705.

Write questions answered by repeating the same number over and over.

```
    1 2 3         1 2 3         1 2 4
  x     2       x     3       x     2
  _____       _____       _____



    1 0 0 0       5 0 0         1 2 4
  x       3     x     3       x     3
  _____     _____       _____
```

MULTIPLICATION BY REPEATED ADDITION WORKSHEET
LET'S TRY SOME MORE!

```
    2 0 0          1 5 0          5 4 4
  x     3        x     3        x     3


    6 0 0          1 7 5          1 5 0
  x     5        x     2        x     7


    2 5 0          2 5 0          2 5 0
  x     3        x     5        x     6
```

MULTIPLICATION BY REPEATED ADDITION WORKSHEET
LET'S TRY EVEN MORE!

```
   3 3 5          3 3 5          3 3 5
 x     2        x     2        x     4


   3 3 5          2 5 0          2 0 0
 x     5        x     4        x     5


   7 0 0          7 0 5          5 0 7
 x     3        x     3        x     3
```

MULTIPLICATION BY AREA

The second concept for multiplication is area. We know the length and width but do not know the total area. An example of an area problem is, "If there are 8 rows and 6 columns of cookies, how many cookies are there all together?"

The simplest way to begin children with area multiplication is to give the children 1-blocks and ask them to make rectangles or squares. In the example below the students count the length and write down 3. Next they count the width and write 2. The final step is to count the total blocks and write the equation 3 x 2=6. Then they add onto these blocks and write another equation. This activity prepares them for the problems to solve on the next page.

The first problems on the next page are simpler and then the 10-blocks are utilized.

Here's a picture of 13 x 5 =

The problems written for children have fewer 1-blocks in order to make the counting easier. One might think that 7 x 9 = is easier than 13 x 5 =. However, the first problem requires young children to count correctly 63 one-blocks while the second problem only has 15 one-blocks to count.

MULTIPLICATION BY AREA WORKSHEET
YOUR TURN!

5 x 2 =   7 x 2 =

6 x 3 =   3 x 4 =

8 x 2 =   6 x 2 =

1 0 x 4 =   1 2 x 4 =

MULTIPLICATION BY AREA WORKSHEET
LET'S TRY SOME MORE!

Draw answers below problems, show 10"s and 1's.

1 2 x 2 =   1 4 x 3 =

1 2 x 4 =   1 3 x 5 =

MULTIPLICATION BY AREA WORKSHEET
LET'S TRY EVEN MORE!

Choose one problem from below to draw, show 10's and 1's.

32 x 3 =   45 x 2 =

45 x 3 =   50 x 5 =

MULTIPLICATION BY AREA WORKSHEET
LET'S TRY EVEN MORE YET!

6 x 5 =

5 x 6 =

1 7 x 9 =

1 1 x 8 =

1 6 x 5 =

5 x 1 6 =

3 2 x 6 =

3 3 x 6 =

DIVVY - UP DIVISION

The first concept for division is divvy-up which is best described as equal sharing. In the earlier problems for students to solve, there are no leftovers and then, the problems include leftovers. At home we call the extras "left-overs" and in school we call them "remainders." The terms are synonymous. It might be helpful in homes to call the items stored after dinner in the refrigerator as the remainders.

One of the first problems is 3693 ÷ 3 =. It may seem crazy for children to have this as an easy division problem, but there is no regrouping and since these students understand place value the problem is very easy. Gather up three 1000-blocks, six 100-blocks, nine 10-blocks, and three 1-blocks. Then children are to share the blocks equally with 3 people. Each person will then have one of the 1000-blocks, two of the 100-blocks, three of the 10-blocks and one of the 1-blocks giving an answer to the division problem of 1,231. Simple. The problems become more complex as regrouping is required.

The picture above is for the problem 1200 ÷ 3 =. The student must exchange the 1000-block for 10-100 blocks and then divide them into 3 piles with each pile having 400.

Write division questions answered by sharing or spreading out evenly. An example is, "A student with an assignment sheet with 25 tasks to complete in the week, can divide 25 into five piles and determine that five tasks per day will finish all of the work."

3)369   3)639

3)963   3)900

3)936   3)906

DIVVY - UP DIVISION WORKSHEET
LET'S TRY SOME MORE!

$3\overline{)3639}$　　　　　$3\overline{)4860}$

$5\overline{)1055}$　　　　　$3\overline{)880}$

$4\overline{)480}$　　　　　$5\overline{)120}$

DIVVY - UP DIVISION WORKSHEET
LET'S TRY EVEN MORE!

Draw answer for one problem below, show 100's, 10's and 1's

$$5 \overline{)565}$$

$$4 \overline{)848}$$

$$3 \overline{)993}$$

$$4 \overline{)520}$$

DIVVY - UP DIVISION WORKSHEET
LET'S TRY EVEN MORE YET!

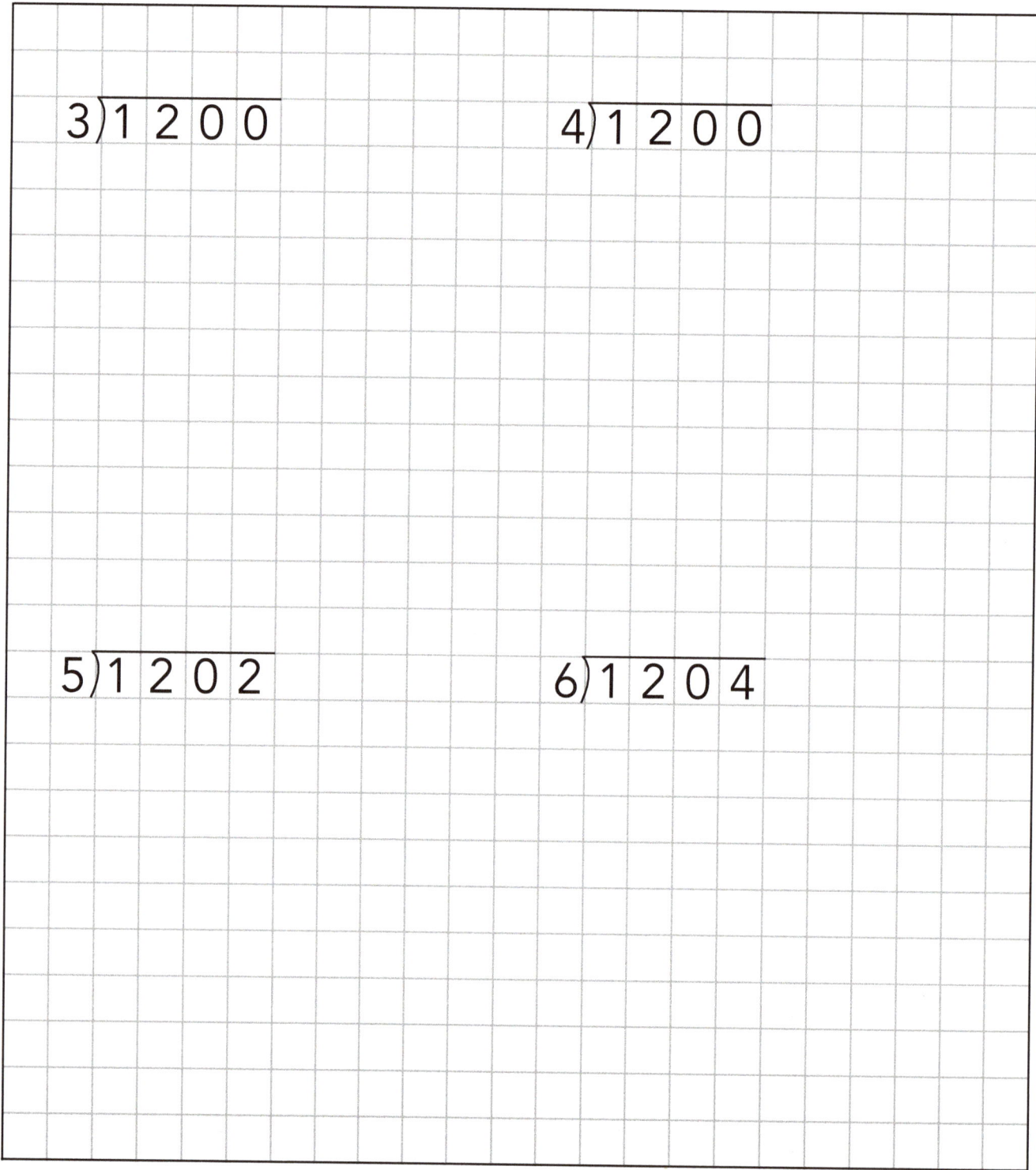

3)1 2 0 0

4)1 2 0 0

5)1 2 0 2

6)1 2 0 4

REPEATED SUBTRACTION DIVISION

The second concept for division is repeated subtraction. There is no sharing like there is for divvy-up division; there is simply the subtracting once, twice, until the original item is gone.

For the problem 848 ÷ 400, the student takes away 400 as many times as possible. The student soon realizes that 400 can only be taken away twice but 48 is left over. The answer is 2 with a remainder of 48. The student can write 2 r48 or 2 with 48 left over. Historically schools use the term remainder and homes use the term leftover. The words are synonyms.

"What's for dinner tonight?" "Remainders." "Huh?"

Write division questions answered by repeated subtraction. A sample question could be, "If I have $20 and a favorite game I like to play that costs $4, how many times can I play the game. I can subtract $4 from my $20 bill five times."

REPEATED SUBTRACTION DIVISION WORKSHEET
YOUR TURN!

How many times can I subtract the divisor from the dividend?
Some problems have leftovers such as 120 ÷ 50.
Write answer as: *2 with 20 leftover, 2 remainder 20, or 2 r 20.*

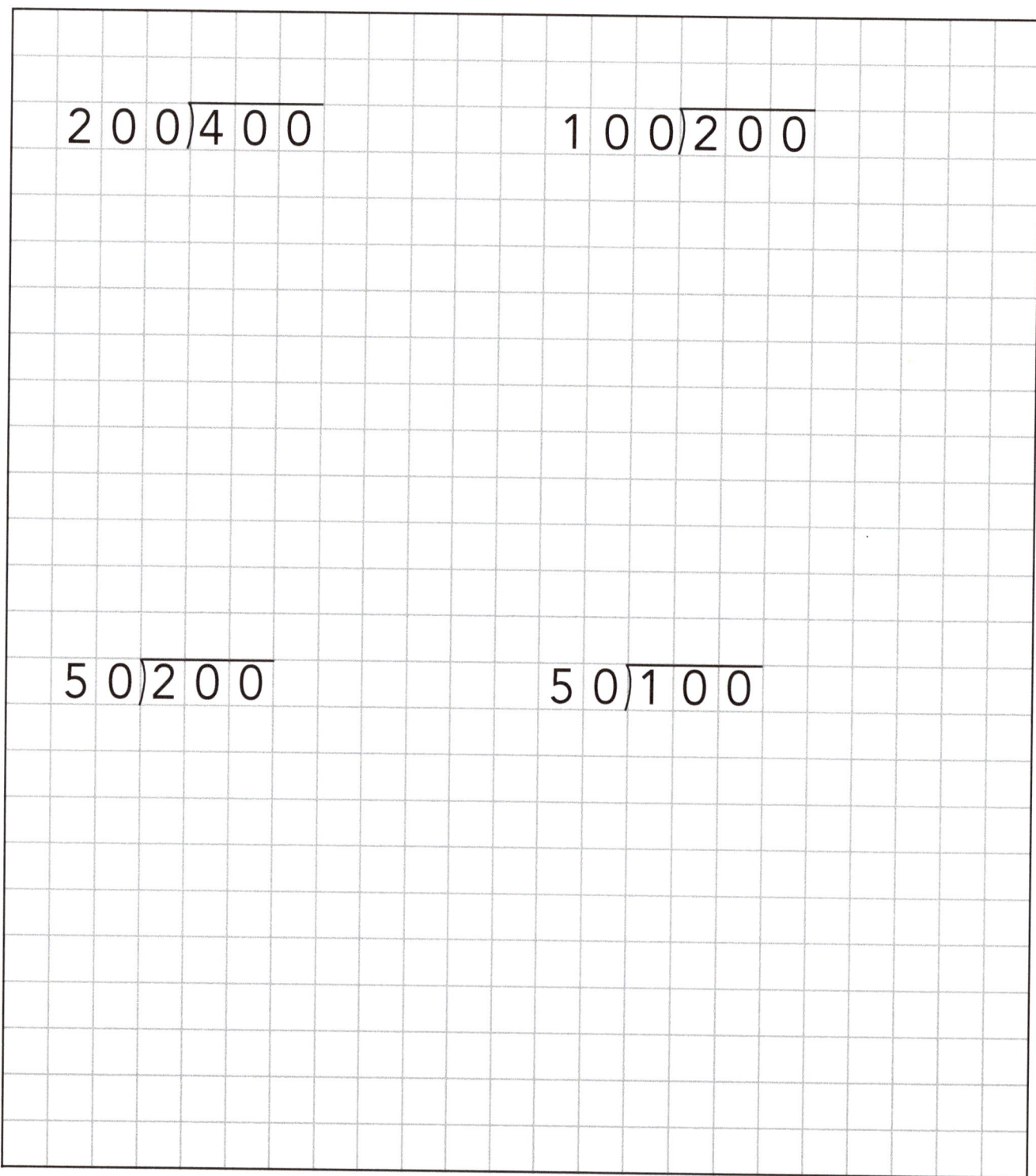

REPEATED SUBTRACTION DIVISION WORKSHEET
LET'S TRY SOME MORE!

How many times can I subtract the divisor from the dividend?
Some problems have leftovers such as 120 ÷ 50.
Write answer as: *2 with 20 leftover, 2 remainder 20, or 2 r 20.*

$$300\overline{)600}$$

$$200\overline{)800}$$

$$250\overline{)1000}$$

$$50\overline{)120}$$

$$300\overline{)1000}$$

$$400\overline{)1000}$$

REPEATED SUBTRACTION DIVISION WORKSHEET
LET'S TRY EVEN MORE!

How many times can I subtract the divisor from the dividend?
Some problems have leftovers such as 120 ÷ 50.
Write answer as: *2 with 20 leftover, 2 remainder 20, or 2 r 20.*

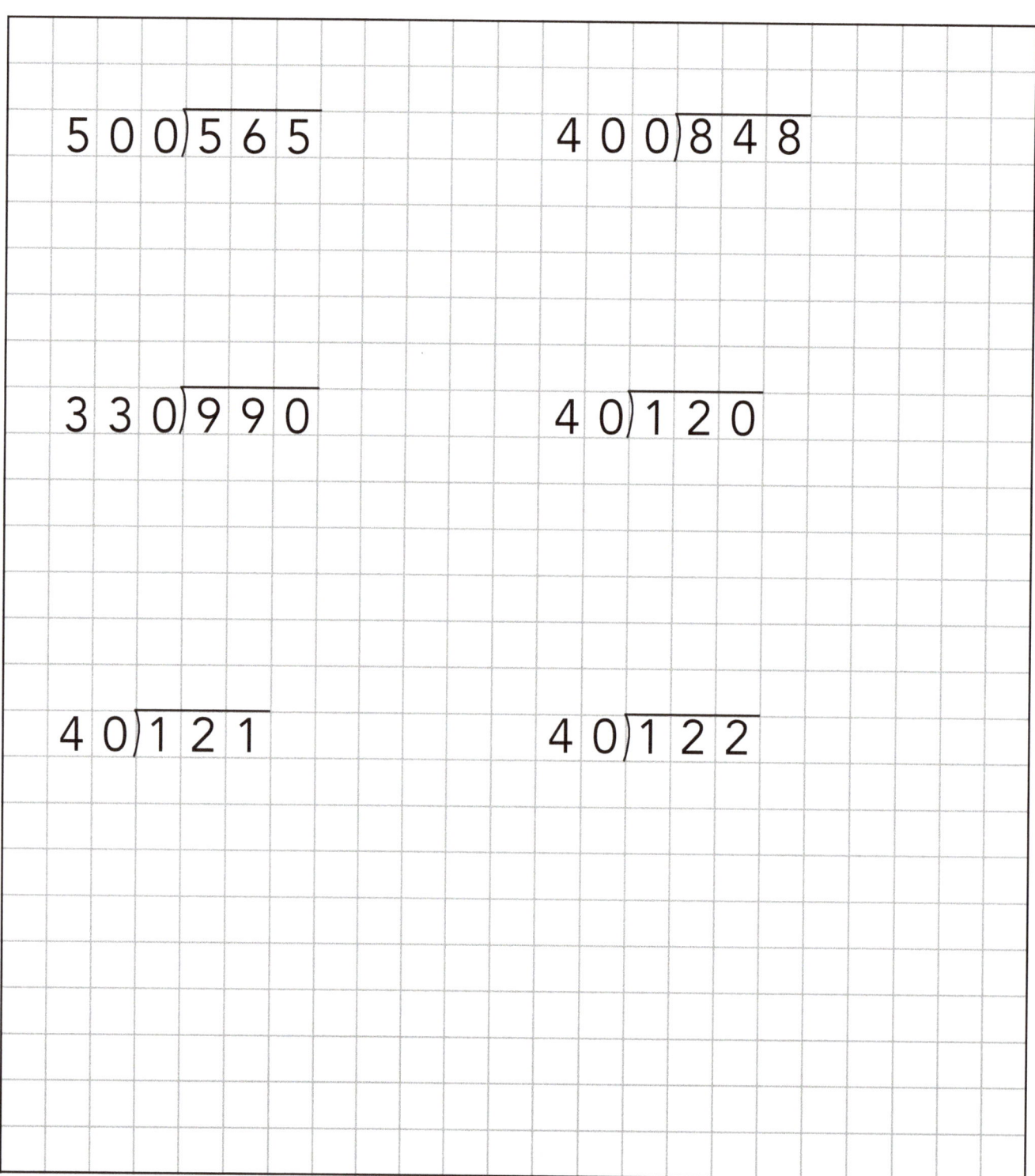

500)565

400)848

330)990

40)120

40)121

40)122

REPEATED SUBTRACTION DIVISION WORKSHEET
LET'S TRY EVEN MORE YET!

How many times can I subtract the divisor from the dividend?
Some problems have leftovers such as 120 ÷ 50.
Write answer as: *2 with 20 leftover, 2 remainder 20, or 2 r 20.*

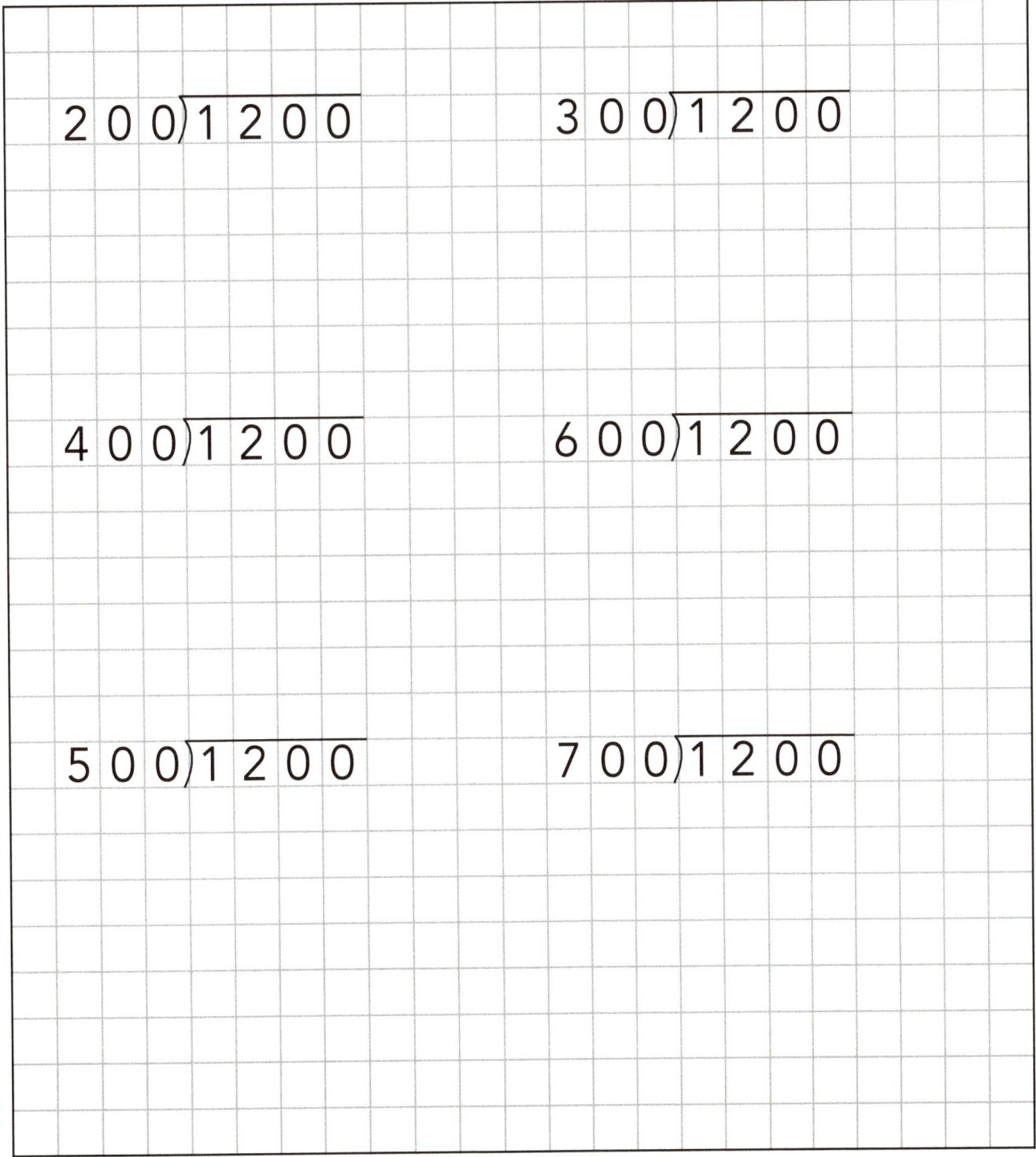

AREA DIVISION

The third concept for division is area. It is very similar to area multiplication where students know the length and the width and the problem is to figure out the area. With division, the student knows the length and the area. The problem is to figure out the width.

For problems such as 132 ÷ 12 = the student is to pick up one 100-block, three 10-blocks and two 1-blocks. They are to put the blocks into a rectangle. One side of the rectangle must measure 12; the adjacent side of the rectangle shows the division answer as 11. Sometimes it will be easier for children to measure the sides of the rectangles with a centimeter ruler although counting the centimeters on the blocks is also quite easy.

Write division questions answered by area. An example is, "I have 16 square feet of flooring. The closet is 5 feet long. What will the width of the flooring be?"

AREA DIVISION WORKSHEET
YOUR TURN!

Each problem below provides the area inside the "L" shape and either the width or the length of a rectangle. Remember, no zig-zags.
Only perfect rectangles allowed for these problems.

1 2$\overline{)3\ 6}$

1 2$\overline{)4\ 8}$

1 2$\overline{)2\ 4}$

8$\overline{)1\ 6}$

1 2$\overline{)1\ 4\ 4}$

1 2$\overline{)1\ 2\ 0}$

AREA DIVISION WORKSHEET
LET'S TRY SOME MORE!

Each problem below provides the area inside the "L" shape and either the width or the
length of a rectangle. Remember, no zig-zags.
Only perfect rectangles allowed for these problems.
Draw all four problems below, show 1's.

2)1 2

4)1 2

3)1 2

6)1 2

Each problem below provides the area inside the "L" shape and either the width or the length of a rectangle. Remember, no zig-zags.
Only perfect rectangles allowed for these problems.

2⟌6 0   3⟌6 0

4⟌8 0   5⟌5 0

1 0⟌6 0   2 0⟌6 0

AREA DIVISION WORKSHEET
LET'S TRY EVEN MORE YET!

Each problem below provides the area inside the "L" shape and either the width or the length of a rectangle. Remember, no zig-zags.
Only perfect rectangles allowed for these problems.
Draw all 4 problems below, show all 10's and 1's.

1 2)2 4

1 2)3 6

1 2)4 8

1 2)7 2

BEYOND +, -, x, ÷
WITH SQUARES AND CUBES

Squares:

For each number, make a square with the blocks and count up the total for the answer.

For example: $2^2 = 4$, read the problem as, "What is 2 squared?"

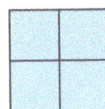

Use the hundred, ten and one blocks for larger problems such as $12^2 = 144$.

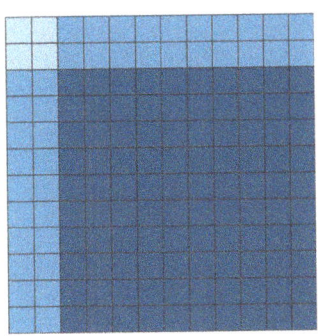

Cubes:

For cubes such as $2^3 = 8$, the problem is to build a cube that is 2 long, 2 wide and 2 high. Then count the total number of blocks. Read the problem as, "What is 2 cubed?"

When solving for, $11^3 = ?$

Use a thousand, hundreds, tens and ones blocks.

The answer is 1,331.

BEYOND +, -, X, ÷
WITH SQUARES AND CUBES WORKSHEET
YOUR TURN!

Draw both square problems below. Take a photo of the cube problems, print and glue on page.

Squares:

$2^2 =$ $3^2 =$

Cubes:

$2^3 =$ $3^3 =$

BEYOND +, -, X, ÷
WITH SQUARES AND CUBES WORKSHEET
LET'S TRY SOME MORE!

Draw both square problems below.

Squares:

$4^2 =$

$10^2 =$

Cubes:

$4^3 =$

$10^3 =$

SQUARES AND CUBES   46

BEYOND +, -, X, ÷
WITH SQUARES AND CUBES WORKSHEET
LET'S TRY EVEN MORE!

Draw a picture of $12^2 =$ below the problems

Squares:

$11^2 =$

$12^2 =$

Cubes:

$11^3 =$

$12^3 =$

BEYOND +, -, x, ÷
WITH SQUARE ROOTS

It would be much simpler for students if the name was square sides instead of square roots. What we are doing is making squares and counting how long the sides are. We will stick with the accurate math term "square roots" but the explanation is all about the length of the sides.

The largest problem on the next page is $\sqrt{961}$ = 31. It is actually quite simple. Make a square with nine 100 - blocks, six 10 - blocks and one 1 - block. Be sure the length and the width of the square are exactly the same.

(If sides are not equal a rectangle or a zig-zag shape has been built instead of a square).

BEYOND +, -, X, ÷
WITH SQUARE ROOTS WORKSHEET
YOUR TURN!

Draw answers to all problems

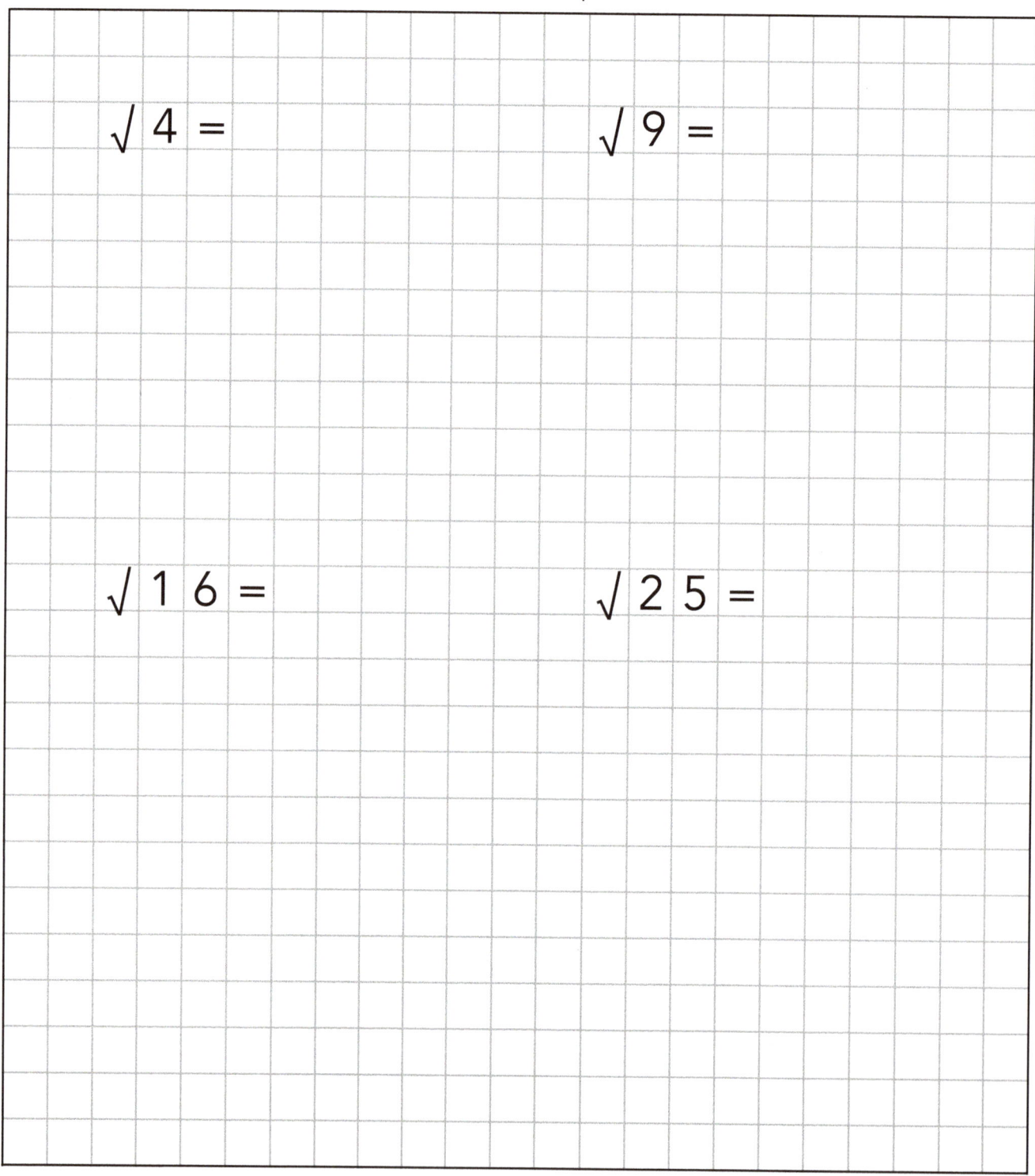

$\sqrt{4} =$

$\sqrt{9} =$

$\sqrt{16} =$

$\sqrt{25} =$

Draw the problem $\sqrt{441}$ below, show 100's, 10's and the 1.

$\sqrt{144} =$ $\sqrt{169} =$

$\sqrt{100} =$ $\sqrt{441} =$

Draw answer to problem √196 =

$\sqrt{121} =$ $\sqrt{961} =$

$\sqrt{484} =$ $\sqrt{196} =$

BEYOND +, -, x, ÷
WITH RECTANGULAR PRISMS

The problems for rectangular prisms are so easy to calculate that it is easy to quickly obtain the answer without any visual picture of the prism. Building with blocks and counting provides the visual that makes the process helpful for future use of the math.

One problem is 6 x 10 x 2 = ?. This means make a rectangular prism that is 6 long, by 10 wide, by 2 high. Use the 10-blocks and 100-blocks as often as possible. The answer can be counted as 120.

$2 \times 3 \times 2 =$

$2 \times 4 \times 2 =$

$2 \times 2 \times 3 =$

$3 \times 2 \times 2 =$

$12 \times 2 \times 2 =$

$12 \times 2 \times 3 =$

$$13 \times 2 \times 2 =$$

$$13 \times 3 \times 3 =$$

$$12 \times 12 \times 2 =$$

$$10 \times 10 \times 3 =$$

$$5 \times 10 \times 2 =$$

$$6 \times 10 \times 2 =$$

5 x 1 0 x 3 =

6 x 1 0 x 3 =

2 0 x 2 x 3 =

3 0 x 2 x 3 =

4 0 x 2 x 3 =

5 0 x 2 x 3 =

TWO-PLACE BY TWO-PLACE MULTIPLICATION

The algorithm most readers were taught in school is to solve the problem 14 x 13 in the manner shown here:

$$\begin{array}{r} 14 \\ \times\ \ 13 \\ \hline 42 \\ +\ \ 140 \\ \hline 182 \end{array}$$

Let's look at this problem with the Base Ten blocks. The algorithm most readers were taught in school is best pictured as an area model. The first line in the partial product, with the method most of us were taught, is one set of the tens plus all of the ones – in this picture is 30 + 12. The second line of the partial product is the 100-block plus the rest of the 10-blocks. We could have been taught to multiply with 4 partial products instead of 2 partial products. It looks like this:

First we multiply 1's by 1's and record all of the 1's (12). Next we multiply 1's by 10's and write down the first group of 10's (30). The third step is to multiply the other 1 by the other 10 to obtain the second group of 10's (40). The fourth line is obtained by multiplying the tens by the tens which gives us 100's. We add up the 4 partial products to obtain the final product of 182.

$$\begin{array}{r} 14 \\ \times\ \ 13 \\ \hline 12 \\ 30 \\ 40 \\ +\ \ 100 \\ \hline 182 \end{array}$$

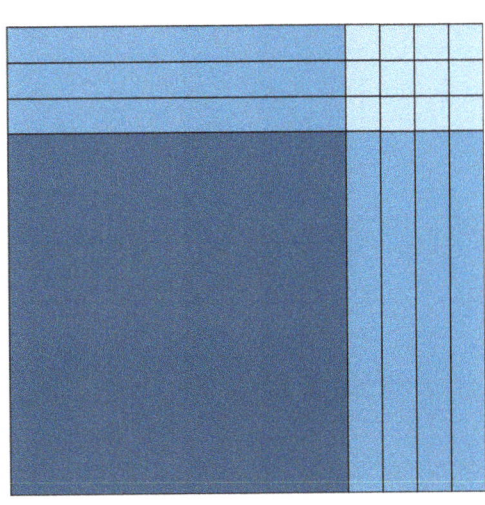

Every 2-place by 2-place multiplication is exactly the same visual with 4 partial products.

Some children will enjoy skipping from 4-partial products to no partial products – they only write down the product. Here's the thinking process using 25 x 31 as an example.

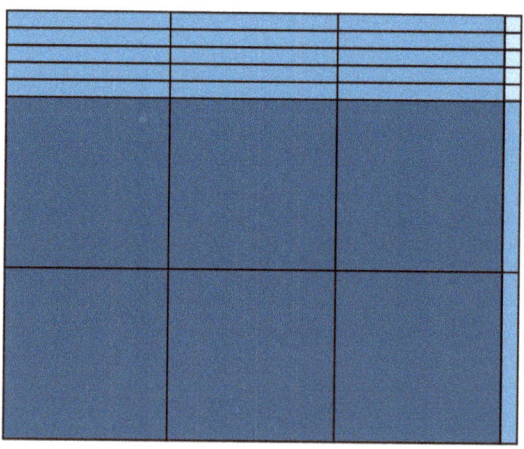

Step 1: Multiply the 1's by the 1's. There are five 1's. Write down 5.

$$
\begin{array}{r}
25 \\
\times\ 31 \\
\hline
5
\end{array}
$$

Step 2: Multiply 1's by 10's which is 1 x 2 tens. Remember 2 tens while you multiply 3 tens x 5 which is 15 more tens giving a total of 17 tens. Write down 7 tens and remember you now have one more 100.

$$
\begin{array}{r}
25 \\
\times\ 31 \\
\hline
75
\end{array}
$$

Step 3: Multiply the tens by tens which will give us 100's. The 3 hundreds times the 2 hundreds gives us six hundreds. Plus we have one hundred to remember from the 17 tens. That's a total of 7 hundreds to record.

$$
\begin{array}{r}
25 \\
\times\ 31 \\
\hline
775
\end{array}
$$

This process of multiplication is not for every student. If students are taught multiplication with 4 partial products most will be pleased to multiply this way. But there are some students in every classroom who love showing adults how to multiply without the bother of partial products.

Here's a practice:

$$\begin{array}{r} 35 \\ \times\ 46 \\ \hline \end{array}$$

Steps:

Multiply 1's times 1's. The answer is 30.

(Write down 0 for the ones and remember you have traded for 3-tens.)

Cross multiply 1's x 10's. You have 18 tens and 20 tens plus 3 to remember. That is 41 tens. Write down 1 ten and remember you have 4 extra 100's.

Multiply 3 tens by 4 tens to obtain twelve 100's. Remember the 4 from multiplying 10's and now you have 16 hundreds.

The answer is 1610.

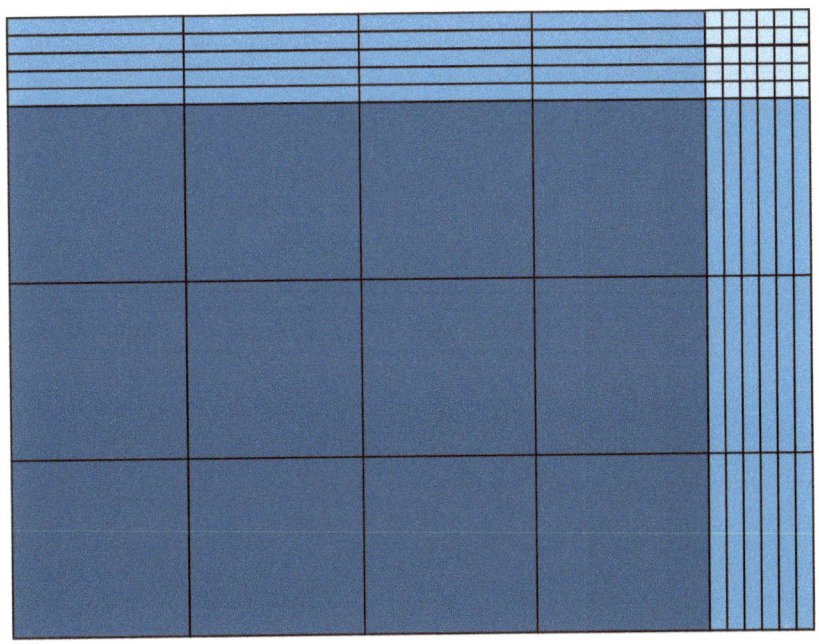

2-PLACE BY 2-PLACE MULTIPLICATION WORKSHEET
YOUR TURN!

Show all four partial products, see example below.

```
    1 1              1 2              1 3
  x 1 1            x 1 2            x 1 3
      1
    1 0
    1 0
+ 1 0 0
  1 2 1


    1 4              1 5              1 6
  x 1 4            x 1 5            x 1 6
```

2-PLACE BY 2-PLACE MULTIPLICATION WORKSHEET
LET'S TRY SOME MORE!

Show all four partial products

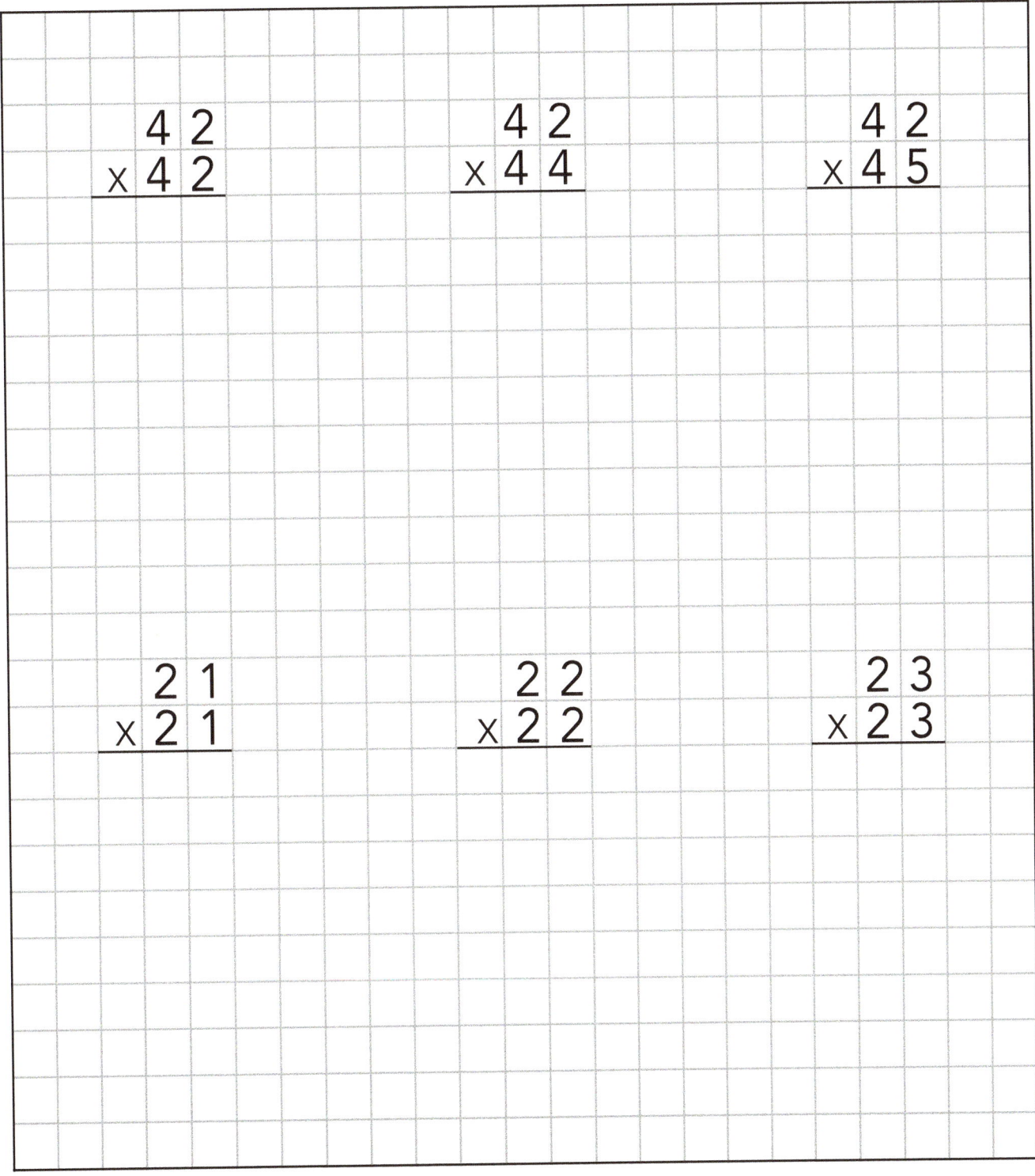

```
    4 2          4 2          4 2
 x  4 2       x  4 4       x  4 5
```

```
    2 1          2 2          2 3
 x  2 1       x  2 2       x  2 3
```

2-PLACE BY 2-PLACE MULTIPLICATION WORKSHEET
LET'S TRY EVEN MORE!

Show all four partial products

```
    2 4              2 5              2 6
  x 2 4            x 2 5            x 2 6
```

```
    2 7              2 1              2 1
  x 2 7            x 2 2            x 2 3
```

2-PLACE BY 2-PLACE MULTIPLICATION WORKSHEET
LET'S TRY EVEN MORE YET!

```
    2 1            2 1            3 2
  x 2 4          x 2 5          x 2 1


    3 2            3 2            3 2
  x 2 2          x 2 3          x 2 5
```

THE DIVISION ALGORITHM IS REPEATED SUBTRACTION

Let's look at a problem together: $32\overline{)800}$

We could solve this problem in a very long time by many, many subtractions. The answer to the problem above is how many times can we take 32 away from 800. Here goes…

$$800 - 32 = 778$$

$$778 - 32 = 746$$

$$746 - 32 = 704$$

$$704 - 32 = 667$$

$$667 - 32 = 635$$

Well, you can see this takes far too long. But the answer can be achieved by going as far as possible and counting up the number of subtractions. People figured out an easier way. It is to subtract ten 32's all at once, which is 320 and then subtract 32's.

Pick up eight 100-blocks and subtract 320 as many times as you can. You can subtract 320 twice. Write down what you subtracted which is 640.

$$
\begin{array}{r}
32\overline{)800} \\
-\ \ 640 \\
\hline
160
\end{array}
$$

160 is left after you take away the 640. Since you cannot subtract anymore 320's start subtracting 32's. You can subtract 32 from 160 five times. The answer to the problem is 25 because you can subtract 320 two times and then 32 five times. Obviously, the aim is to move away from the blocks and divide with pencil and paper alone. It takes some bit of practice with the blocks before children gradually internalize the numbers and quickly divide. They do not need to remember steps to follow; they know the steps with the blocks.

Here is another problem:

$$12\overline{)2532}$$

In this problem the student can take away a hundred 12's at once which is 1200

Next the student takes away ten 12's at once which is 120

Finally, the student takes away 12's.

$$12\overline{)2532}$$

−	2400	Take away 1200 two times
	132	is left
−	120	Now take away 120's. Only one 120 can be subtracted
	12	is left
−	12	After subtracting 100 12's at once and then 10 12's at once
	0	There is only one step left - subtract 12's

The last example: 321 with 7 left over

$$25\overline{)8032}$$

−	7500	take away 2500 three times.
	532	
−	500	take away 250 twice
	32	
−	25	take away 25 one time
	7	left over

We could use a calculator to actually take 25 away from 8032 over and over. We would be exhausted after 321 times of subtracting – even with a calculator. So much easier to understand how the algorithm most of us were taught was invented.

THE DIVISION ALGORITHM IS
REPEATED SUBTRACTION WORKSHEET
YOUR TURN!

15)3600

☐ Take away 1500's
☐ Take away 150's
☐ Take away 15's

15)360

☐ Take away 150's
☐ Take away 15's

THE DIVISION ALGORITHM IS
REPEATED SUBTRACTION WORKSHEET
LET'S TRY SOME MORE!

$$12\overline{)3600}$$

$$12\overline{)360}$$

$$15\overline{)2530}$$

$$12\overline{)3730}$$

$$12\overline{)253}$$

$$12\overline{)373}$$

$$15\overline{)1572}$$

$$12\overline{)1572}$$

BEYOND +, -, x, ÷
WITH SQUARE/CUBE ROOTS AGAIN

It is easy to visualize square roots such as √9, √16, or even √64. The square root of 9 is created by placing 9 blocks and counting that the four sides are all 3 long. Likewise the square roots of 16 and 64 can be visualized by creating the picture in your mind of a square with 16 blocks and another square with 64 blocks. Counting the length of the sides gives answers of 4 and 8 for the square roots.

However, visualizing √10 is not so easy because ten blocks cannot be arranged into a square. We can make a 3 x 3 square, but one block is left over.

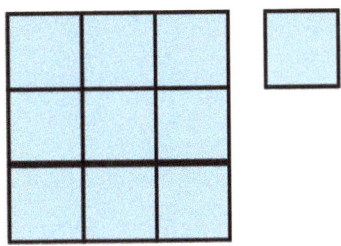

Let's personify the blocks. Assume that the 3 x 3 square aspires to become a 4 x 4 square. How many more of the little 1-blocks does the 3 x 3 square need? He needs 7 more. So the square root of 10 is approximately 3 1/7 because with ten blocks we can make a 3 x 3 square and also we are 1/7 of the way to becoming a 4 x 4 square.

The pattern continues:

√11 ≈ 3 2/7

√12 ≈ 3 3/7

√13 ≈ 3 4/7

√14 ≈ 3 5/7

√15 ≈ 3 6/7

√16 = 4

Just like the 3 x 3 square had aspirations to become a 4 x 4 square the 8 x 8 square has the desire to become a 9 x 9 square. If we have 70 blocks, we can make an 8 x 8 square with 64 of them and have 6 left over. It takes 17 more blocks to grow from an 8 x 8 square into a 9 x 9 square. In the picture below we observe that it is easy to see it takes 17. In order to turn an 8 x 8 square into a 9 x 9 we add 8 blocks onto one side and 8 on the bottom. That is 16 blocks but then we need to add one in the corner to have a total of 17.

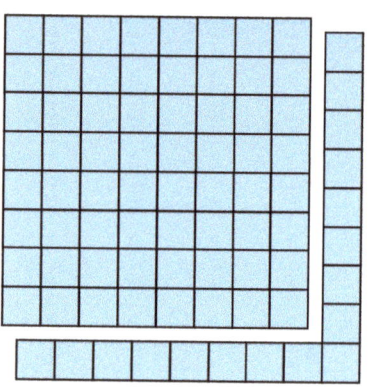

The square root of 70 is approximately 8 and 6/17.

Some of the simplest problems are those that are over 100 because so few blocks are needed. Let's take, for example, $\sqrt{105} \approx$ ___. We can picture this as 1-hundred block with five 1-blocks left over. So, the next question is how many blocks do we have to add to a 10 x 10 square to become an 11 x 11 square. It takes 21 blocks more to change a 10 x 10 square into an 11 x 11 square. And since we have 105 blocks, the square root of 105 is approximately 10 and 5/21.

The approximation with the blocks is very close to the actual square root. To compare use a calculator to find out the decimal equivalent of 5/21. It is 0.238. So, our approximate square root of 105 is 10.238. With the same calculator we can find out the precise square root of 105. It is 10.246. With simple blocks we are off by only .008 – amazing.

The exact same process works for cube root estimation. What is the cube root of 10? The largest cube that can be made with ten 1-blocks is 2 x 2 x 2 which takes eight 1-blocks and leaves two 1-blocks. I hope readers now understand the process. How many more 1-blocks does it take to turn a 2 x 2 x 2 block into a 3 x 3 x 3 block? It takes 19. Thus the cube root of 10 is approximately 2 2/19th. What about the cube root of 1020? Start with a 1000 block and build an 11 x 11 x 11 block. How many more blocks are needed to turn a 10 x 10 x 10 into an 11 x 11 x 11? Go for it!

BEYOND +, -, X, ÷
WITH SQUARE/CUBE ROOTS WORKSHEET
YOUR TURN!

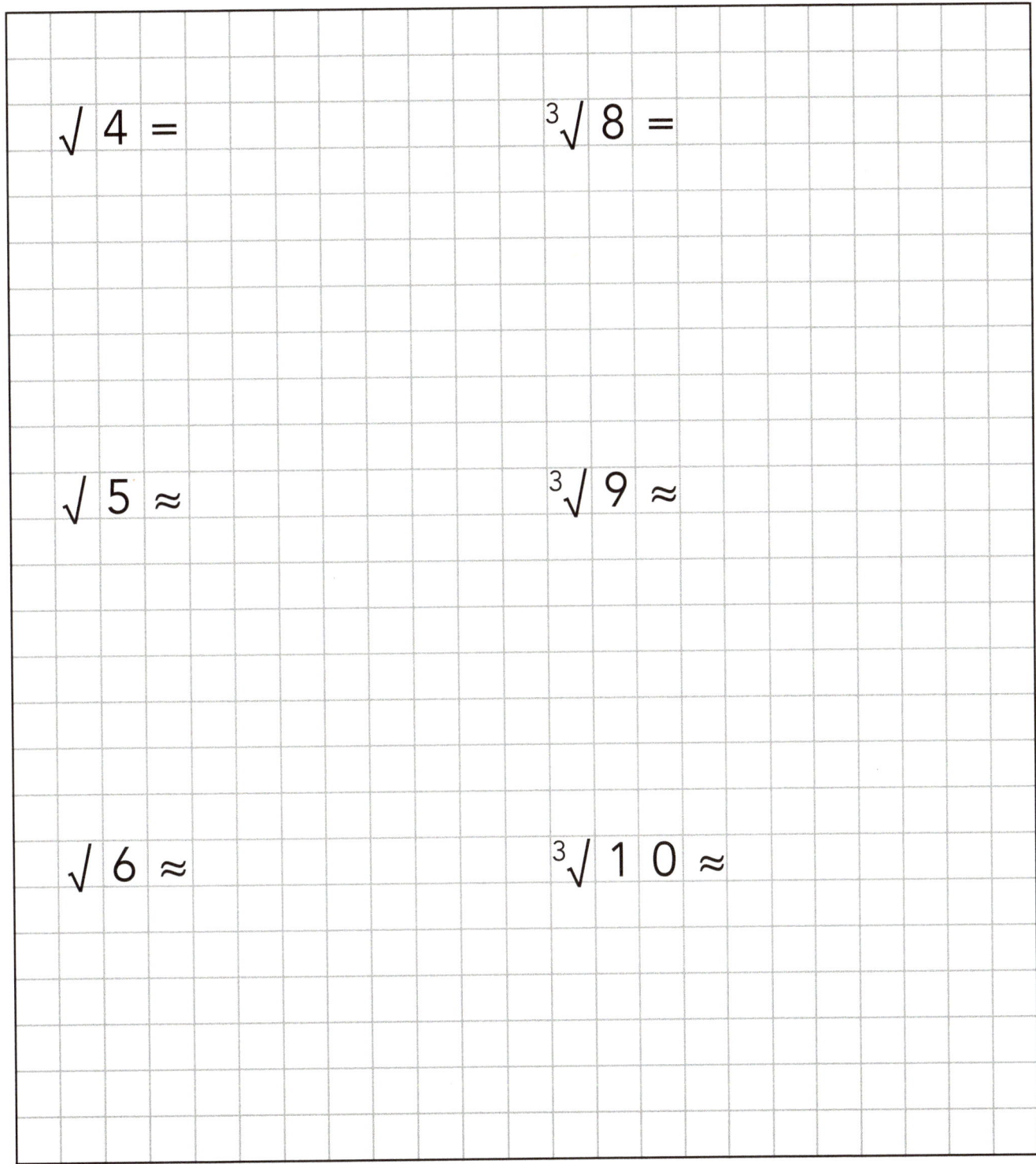

$\sqrt{4} =$

$\sqrt[3]{8} =$

$\sqrt{5} \approx$

$\sqrt[3]{9} \approx$

$\sqrt{6} \approx$

$\sqrt[3]{10} \approx$

$\sqrt{7} \approx$

$\sqrt[3]{12} \approx$

$\sqrt{8} \approx$

$\sqrt[3]{13} \approx$

$\sqrt{9} =$

$\sqrt[3]{27} =$

$\sqrt{10} \approx$

$\sqrt[3]{35} \approx$

$\sqrt{11} \approx$

$\sqrt[3]{50} \approx$

$\sqrt{12} \approx$

$\sqrt[3]{64} =$

$\sqrt{13} \approx$ $\sqrt[3]{30} \approx$

$\sqrt{14} \approx$ $\sqrt[3]{1000} =$

$\sqrt{15} \approx$ $\sqrt[3]{1001} \approx$

BEYOND +, -, X, ÷
WITH SQUARE/CUBE ROOTS WORKSHEET
LET'S TRY A WHOLE BUNCH MORE!

$\sqrt{17} \approx$ $\sqrt[3]{11} \approx$

$\sqrt{100} =$ $\sqrt[3]{1002} \approx$

$\sqrt{101} \approx$ $\sqrt[3]{1003} \approx$

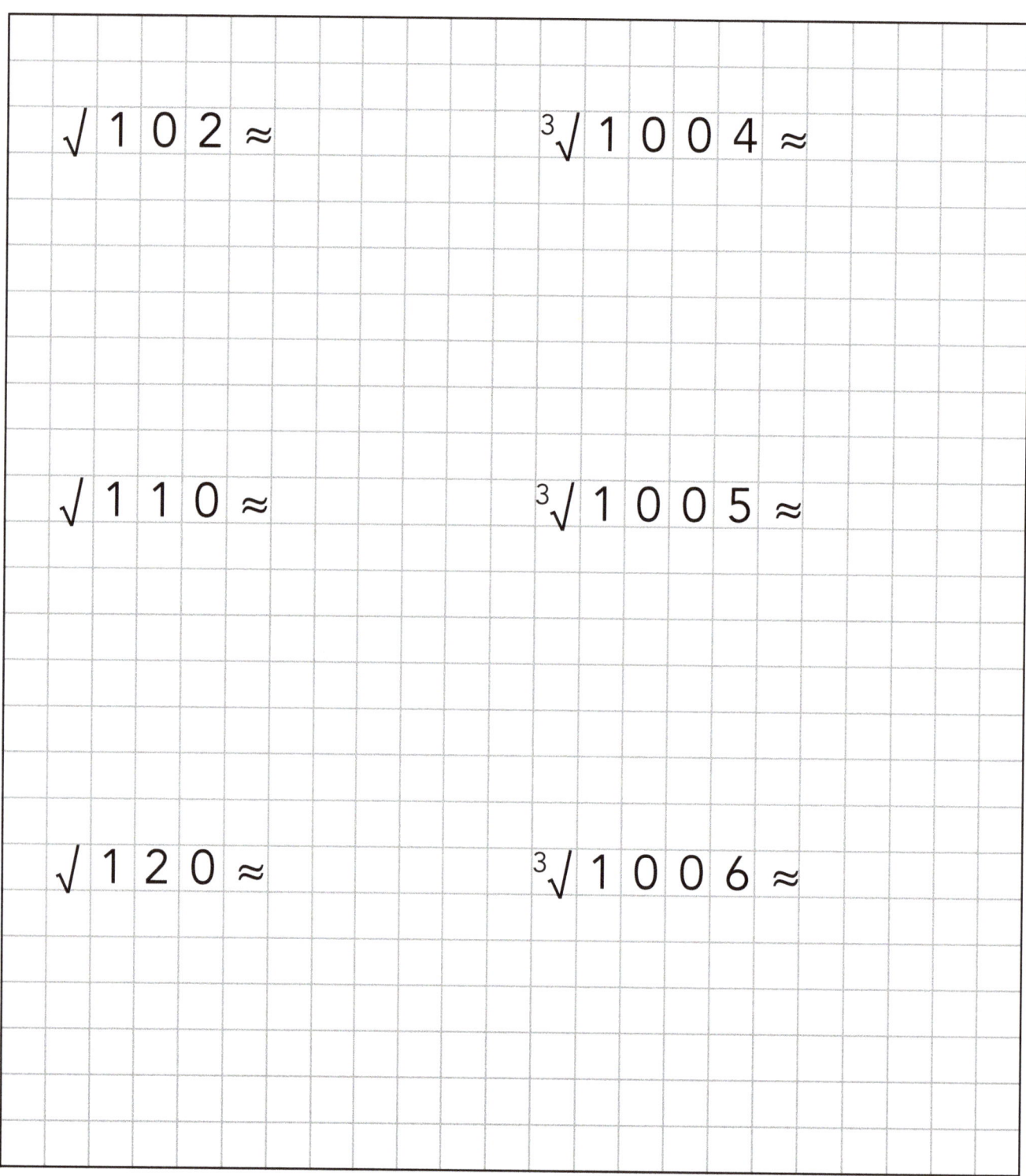

$\sqrt{102} \approx$ $\sqrt[3]{1004} \approx$

$\sqrt{110} \approx$ $\sqrt[3]{1005} \approx$

$\sqrt{120} \approx$ $\sqrt[3]{1006} \approx$

$\sqrt{16} =$

$\sqrt[3]{1007} \approx$

$\sqrt{445} \approx$

$\sqrt[3]{1008} \approx$

$\sqrt{965} \approx$

$\sqrt[3]{1009} \approx$

ABOUT THE AUTHOR

Dr. Lyle Lee Jenkins is an author, speaker, and recognized authority in improving educational outcomes. He believes that implementing a growth mindset and celebrating progress are the keys to helping students learn more and retain their enthusiasm for school.

His education experience, that spans over 50 years, ranges from working as a teacher, a principal, and a school superintendent to being a University Professor. In 2003, Lyle Lee founded LtoJ, LLC hoping to impact and guide the way we approach education.

Lyle Lee Jenkins has authored six books showcasing continuous improvement in schools, including *How to Create a Perfect School, Optimize Your School, Permission to Forget, From Systems Thinking to Systemic Action, Improving Student Learning*, and *How to Create a Perfect Home School*. All literature offers powerful, practical suggestions for every aspect of education. The two most influential people supporting Dr. Jenkins's work are W. Edwards Deming and John Hattie.

Having spoken to educators all across the United States, and into Latin America, Europe, Australia, and Asia, Lyle Lee Jenkins is passionate about equipping the next generation with a true love of learning.

Dr. Lyle Lee Jenkins holds a Bachelor of Arts degree from Point Loma Nazarene University, a Masters of Education from San Jose State University and a Ph.D. from The Claremont Graduate University.

Lyle Lee Jenkins's website, www.LtoJ.net, is a great place to discover useful tools to guide your educational journey.

Purchasers of *How to Create Math Experts with Base Ten Blocks* by Lyle Lee Jenkins may utilize this QR code to download worksheets from this book at no extra cost. This will ease the process of making copies for individual students. Both the print and downloaded copies are protected by copyright laws.